EXISTENTIAL

ORA SOHUM

This work is dedicated to the Universe and all contained within it.

Contents

Preface *vii*

Acknowledgements *ix*

1. A Grain Of Sand 1
2. Anxiety Attacks 3
3. Aries 5
4. Asteroid 6
5. Best Bloody Scenario 7
6. Broken, Shattered And Torn 9
7. Burn Your Bridges 11
8. Die 13
9. End Of The Rope (back To The Pain) 15
10. Evolution Regression 17
11. Face Your Fears 19
12. For A Reason, For A Season 21
13. Grew Up Screwed Up 23
14. Grief 26
15. I Dream Of Stars 28
16. I'm Ok, I'm Fine 29
17. It Doesn't Matter 31
18. Pain Fall Down 34
19. Painkillers 36
20. Reminisce 38
21. Sex On The Weekend 40
22. Silver 43

Contents

23. Special Needs 45

24. State Of Starvation 47

25. Step Outside 48

26. Stop Sexualizing Me 50

27. The Flow 53

28. The Hours 54

29. There's Me 55

30. Today 58

31. Trigger 59

Preface

As a young child, starting from the age of 6, when we had to pen our first composition in school, I put pencil to paper and wrote just 5 lines on My Dog. I didn't have a dog. I barely knew how to spell, forget about trying to string words together for coherency.

When emotions started getting in the way of life as a blossoming child, and when I was prevented from expressing it at all by adults at home, in society and at school, the only way that I could spew out what was bubbling inside, was to self medicate by the use of pen and paper.

Life can sometimes appear complex, and I wasn't mature at the time to first be aware of, then understand and finally cope with stages of growth, coupled with the onslaught of constant trauma and chaos.

Over the years, I've written hundreds of lines, sometimes at the back of school notebooks, on tissue paper, loose sheets and Word documents. They always reflected what was brewing inside my head, always existential questions that I hadn't yet found the answers to. Some of what I've written has been lost - either torn up, burnt, trashed or confiscated by my parents, who were absolutely against me expressing creativity in any form.

No matter what the output, no matter the result, no matter the medium, there is one beautiful facet to being human - imagination. It's what allows us to go beyond what is in front of us, what is inside of us, and escape into an infinite universe of possibilities. I treasure this aspect about us, this gift to imagine, for without it, I wouldn't be where I am, I wouldn't even be alive.

Because I knew only darkness since I could comprehend as an infant, most of my early work focused around depressive subjects, including suicidal thoughts and the eagerness to self-inflict more pain, if it wasn't already being meted out by someone else. Then came the rebellion of my teens and early twenties, when I felt I could physically escape and do away with the abuse once and for all.

Life started to simmer down, after I decided to dissect the trauma and its after-effects, make better choices for myself, and realize that even though I play a miniscule role on the Universal stage, I am still allowed to shine as bright as the sun. Who knows what will come next? In each and every one of my works, I always stitch a little part of me into it. It's the only legacy I wish to have.

I've sorted the poetry in upcoming pages, in alphabetical order. You can flip or scroll through them however you want and interpet each word, each line, in whatever way you want. I leave it up to your imagination.

Ora Sohum
ora.sohum@gmail.com

Acknowledgements

I would like to thank every one who came into my life for a reason, for a season.

I would also like to thank NASA, whose photograph of a black hole is also the cover of this book.

1. A GRAIN OF SAND

What am I?
Only a grain of sand
Stumbling on the shores of eternity
One with the cosmic plan

Time and space
Is a concept of relativity
Fibonacci, the spiral
Swirling in the far-flung arm of the galaxy

The fickle human mind, a shadow of the iridescent soul
Hurtling through existence
Post mortem engulfed, embraced
Reborn in the womb of the black hole

When the final breath of earthly life
Escapes from me
Diving, free falling
I will, into the depths of the cosmic sea

Sailing for an eternity on the microwaves
From the big bang

I AM at one
With the cosmic plan

2. ANXIETY ATTACKS

Innocence, can you keep a secret?
I'll never hurt you, but they didn't mean it
Round and round in a downward spiral
Labyrinth of caution, paranoia
Self-loathing, self-harm, mutilating
Outward scars, inner – I'm festering
Blinding darkness, find my way out
Slipping into an abyss of self-doubt

Another day
Of being judged, stared at
Judged
Because of who you are
Of feeling haunted
There's a demon sitting on my head
Of paranoia, of panic
Of hearing a sound of the past that once triggered violence
Of being misunderstood
Because no one will take the time to understand
Of living
Though waiting to die
The opposite of sober

I am a coward
Every sound is suffocating me
Yet the silence screams menacingly in my ears
Another day
Another battle fought

3. ARIES

I know a boy born of fire
And he burned in me a ravenous desire
His embrace was shelter, his breath was warmth
And I leapt heart-first into the eyes of his storm

I know a boy with a hundred smiles
But the one I loved best was the one that was mine
With his spade tongue he dug in me
A well of pleasure like ecstasy

I know a boy with a broken past
He spews turbulent words but has a tender heart
And the scent of him is intoxicating
And the thought of losing him is excruciating

I know a boy I could love so well
If only he'd evolve from his stifling shell
But he ran away with what was left of me
And now I'm buried deep in agony

4. ASTEROID

Fathomed into existence by cosmic lust
Composed of cosmic gas and dust
Free fall, free fall, inevitably rust

Orbiting on wanderer's lonely quest
Then gravity of hearts cause to coalesce
Collision by astrological hex

Our paths consist of mysteries
Roving satellite in swirling galaxy
Our purpose is but a fallacy

The brevity of our dream
Time tends to warp reality
We exist only momentarily

The destiny of asteroid
In defining moment, destroyed
Fading into oblivion, into the void

5. BEST BLOODY SCENARIO

I have them with their faces to the wall
Bound hands behind their backs in the hall
Weakness blatant in their eyes of fear
Flesh of my flesh, how did we get here?

Screams once echoed in this edifice –
My bloodcurdling cries in response to a fist
And their loud accusations, oh how I reminisce
I'll silence it forever with my blade's kiss

I am momentarily enraged by pathetic plea
A feeble attempt at a pardoned release
And startling reminder to remember my place
Theirs will be on this floor, if I make haste

So I make my decision to finalize their fate
I'll be at rest once I quench this hate
Take the fatal swing betwixt bated breath
Breathe a sigh of relief at the crescendo of their death

I allow them to make their final request
"But you cannot choose life," I say in jest
They beg for forgiveness in their final hour
With blade I promise, "Any moment now"

There's a split-second commotion in the final act
A crimson smile bleeding from the rigid neck
Mortal your remains, immortal my pain
I was dead inside, long before you were slain

As paleness shrouds the fallen corpses
There is no more brutality from the rigor mortis
I am hellishly aroused by this morbidity
Then by my own hand, I set myself free

6. BROKEN, SHATTERED AND TORN

Somehow, I knew that this would be the end
You never really were my friend
I gathered all my strength, and I was reborn;
But I cannot kiss the world again
I have no love left to defend
You left me defenceless, wounded and feeling

Broken, shattered and torn

You raped me and left me naked to die
You caught my beating heart in your hand
You slit me open
And I bled on and on;
You threatened me with hateful words
You knew how much it would hurt
But you continued, and now I am

Broken, shattered and torn

You bound me and hid me from the world
You burned my dreams into dust
You left me in the dark
And I was forlorn;
You banged my face into the wall
You tortured me, but that's not all
You kicked me into the ground and left me

Broken, shattered and torn

You wormed your way into my brain, and left me insane
You're sadistic and you enjoy my pain
You were all, everything I had
And when you were done, you were gone;
I had no one on my side
I only had hope that didn't yet die
I called out to the fractured sky, I was now

Broken, shattered and torn

7. BURN YOUR BRIDGES

Get out of your home
Get out of your comfort zone
It's never easy, but it's fun
When you make it on your own

Grab your pitchforks
Get all that you've got
These prison walls were built with no thought
To an impending revolt

Throw out the sulphur
The smouldering hate
Get rid of all the shit and with it
Throw out all of the shame
Break out of all of it
The bonds of the time
The abyss of mediocrity
The depressing times of life

Make up your mind

And don't be afraid
It is no wonder
That you've always been different
If you don't fit in
It's because you were never meant to be
Do what you want to do
That's when you'll be free

If you don't get love
If it is tough
Burn your bridges
Forget all this shit
If you feel wasted
Unappreciated
Start up a fire, burn your bridges
No going back to it

8. DIE

Like a wish
Like a dream
You were my
Happiest memory;
I try to gaze
Upon your vague face
Scattered images
I try to relive

I'd do anything to touch you again
My eternal friend

How do you think it made me feel
To watch you go?
It is now so hard to breathe
I'd like to let you know
That I'm here, forced to live
Till I'm with you again, I'll exist
I'm so broken
But I won't cry
I can't believe I lived
To see you die

Your ashen remains
I want to exhume
Taste it on my tongue
As I'm consumed
You were my
Intoxicating perfume
Now I'm the living dead
In this embodied tomb

For eternity, I want to be with you; without you, life is cursed
I can't wait to die after you; in your afterglow, I'm immersed

9. END OF THE ROPE (BACK TO THE PAIN)

Oh, I'm back to the pain
My heart, broken again
I thought I was healed of this mental disease
Then a ton of bricks falls on me
And I can't breathe;
Oh, I reel from the pain
So hollow inside, the tears don't run again
Feel like I'm at the end of the rope
The one I tried to hang from before
And I'm alone

I live in a house of glass
They keep throwing stones, I keep bringing up the past
The wounds fester as I keep sucking at the gashes
Waiting for the day I'm interned to ashes
As my world crashes;
I'm desolate and abandoned
Took my beating heart for granted
They told me it was better if I hadn't been born
I hate how we've regressed

Life is a mess
Broken fetters, but they're tighter on my mind
Don't remember me when I've died

10. EVOLUTION REGRESSION

The story of Sapiens began 70,000 years ago
When they first stood erect on East Africa's shore

And set their sights on the North and further East
Where they began to conquer both land and beast

But the Earth's abundance was not enough
Man's heart filled with greed, his loins with lust

So with fire and blood, lay death in his dust
And he considered his wrath to be just

Then industry and coin made him wealthy
During the Renaissance of Rousseau and Machiavelli

And Machiavellian was his plan to dominate State
Charlatans crowned, puritans burnt at the stake

In our age, we are bound by law and screens
Have we really evolved from our history?

Weak men have created weapons for arms
Fighters for justice are caged on a false charge

As fragile minds bow before a deity
And the corrupt hide under a veil of piety

Fiction is worshipped, fact is denied
Liars are godhead, truth seekers are crucified

You say your hate is different from another's
You believe your sisters are weaker than your brothers

And the race to outer space is billionaire's gold
Still empty remains the beggar's bowl

It is not lost to time, this Homo Sapiens history
It is being proliferated through madness and machinery

11. FACE YOUR FEARS

When you want to run
Before your feet hit the floor
You're giving up

Face your fears

Sometimes you're scared
Your heart's filled with dread
It's all in your head

Face your fears

And when you silently cry
Thinking you'd rather die
Than ever try

Face your fears

Trying to walk out the door
Feel you can't take it anymore
You don't know what's yet in store

Face your fears

Do you feel alone?
Intoxicated to feel like you belong
But your heart is worn

Face your fears

Pick yourself up again
Dust all doubt away
Try again

Release, believe, breathe
Face your fears

12. FOR A REASON, FOR A SEASON

Dear old friends and acquaintances,
How are you doin' today?
I hope that life has brought what you asked for
I believe you're blessed, like I prayed
The road of life had once brought us together
But we drove on at our own pace
And I cherish all that you left behind for me
The lessons learnt, the memories, the mistakes

You came into my life for a reason, for a season
You brought me on the path that may have changed me, that I'm still living
The loss and gain, and the joy and the pain
The scars remind me that I'm still hoping
You came into my life for a reason, for a season

Dearly departed friends and family
How are you doin' in heaven?
My tears may have dried, though I'd still die to meet you
Knowing I'll see you again, makes me feel better

Before you left me, like you did so suddenly
You gave me love I wouldn't have ever known
But whenever I looked in your eyes, though it was no surprise to me
You were an angel sent here by God

You came into my life for a reason, for a season
You brought me on the path that may have changed me, that I'm still living
The loss and gain, and the joy and the pain
The scars remind me that I'm still hoping
You came into my life for a reason, for a season

13. GREW UP SCREWED UP

We are the lovechild of hate
We'd rather masturbate
Than express ourselves freely;
Frustrated, so complicated
With dicks in our hand
Waving the white flag, procrastinating

I can't blame you for being a whore
Your father stumbling, drunken, through the door
The welts from the belt leaving you sore
As you cover your ears from their loud voices
And you close your eyes to avoid the bruises
Further violence is what you anticipated

The truth is a bitter pill to swallow
You'd rather take drugs than talk about your sorrow
You're safe where you hide in denial's shadow

We grew up screwed up
Our fate is twisted

Who we could have been
If we resisted
And the train away from pain
But we missed it
We grew up screwed up
Is there still a way to fix it?

Who knows what went on in your childhood
The monster you became is still misunderstood
Mommy crying in the dark in a corner
Too self-absorbed to care about her daughter
So to raise some hell we come home way too late
We can't cope with their chastisement, we're too cross-faded
Light another cigarette near the open window
Throw all evidence in the trash so they'll never know

You're stuck at the age of your deepest trauma
You loathe as much as you crave the psycho drama
You survive twice a day, flatline from the marijuana

We grew up screwed up
Our fate is twisted
Who we could have been
If we resisted
And the train away from pain
But we missed it
We grew up screwed up

Is there still a way to fix it?

In your mind, you've created a fantasy
Because you're ashamed of your poverty
And you'll never bring the girl back home
You make an excuse about why your shirt is torn

You're two-faced, you're a victim and an asshole
Carrying the weight, you pretend you don't care anymore
If only life turned out different for you and me
If only the adults man up and take responsibility

There is no outcome, no end, no repentance
This is our story, this is our life sentence
To be deformed, to be society's rejects, a menace

We grew up screwed up
Our fate was twisted
Who we could have been
If we resisted
And the train away from pain
But we missed it
We grew up screwed up
Is there still a way to fix it?

14. GRIEF

Since when did the night fall
Like a veil over the day?
The clock ticks slowly
In an absent-minded way

Bereaved over my beloved
Over what wasn't meant to be
Oh, it is so unfortunate
You are not my destiny

Amongst the ashes of my fantasy
A gravesite to our demise
A fool I was, twice bitten
I was wounded, yet now I am wise

And scalded by the rejection
Of my own fervent prayer
In solace I can contemplate
Wither eventually, without you there

My grief is an ocean
Washes my soul in gentle laps

Then like angry sea in motion
Crushes my will, perhaps

A flame may burn, but for a while
Turns to bitter, blackened truth
I must let the grief fade like the tide
I'll be better off without you

15. I DREAM OF STARS

I don't remember when I last saw the moon
I get caught up by the day, usually by noon

And holding me in are walls and ceilings
Confining me with my dreams, thoughts and feelings

The sky always seems so unreachable to me
So I capture the constellations in my dreams

Maybe one day I'll be lying in the grass
Humming, looking up at the stars

And my heart will fly like a bird soaring high
To meet with the stars in the magnificent sky

And hopefully it will be when I'm alive and still filled with mirth
Not when my eyes are closed forever and I'm looking up from under earth

16. I'M OK, I'M FINE

There's a place I know too well
And sometimes, I fall under its spell

It's so dark there, I can't see the truth
So I dig deeper to hide from you

All alone in this abyss
My mind slowly begins to play tricks

It tells me I'll never get out
No one will hear me, no matter how loud I shout

It says that I deserve to be where I am
That no matter how hard I try, I'll never stand a chance

It magnifies all of my mistakes
It stops me from making an escape

Playing on repeat is a symphony
That I'm not even worth your pity

So I begin to think that maybe I should stay

And hope that the voices will go away

I take shelter in what I consider familiar
That the world will not notice and I will remain here

But just I begin to get used to the pain
A light flickers and I'm trying again

17. IT DOESN'T MATTER

My bowl overflowed to make sure I was filled
I was slaving too hard for a commercial skill
Breaking my back and my mind for the bills
And what for?
Overthinking about what others think of me
Plotting revenge on those who hurt me
Crying over those who never wanted me
And what for?

When the lights go out
What will be left of me?
A past I can't take back
And my legacy
So all the times I filled with anger, misery and jealousy
It doesn't matter

All the money I had
That can't be spent
On the time that I had
To get closer to friends

So all the time I wasted on sadness and worry
It doesn't matter

Following paths made by someone else
Falling for someone before I love myself
Living each day just to build up on wealth
And what for?
Mouthing a prayer that I don't really mean
Hurting my brother because of my insecurity
Pretending to be anyone, because I'm afraid to be me
And what for?

When the lights go out
What will be left of me?
A past I can't take back
And my legacy
So all the times I filled with anger, misery and jealousy
It doesn't matter

All the money I had
That can't be spent
On the time that I had
To get closer to friends
So all the time I wasted on sadness and worry
It doesn't matter

What really matters to me?

Maybe my comfort and my sanity
And of all those who never gave up on me
The rest doesn't matter

18. PAIN FALL DOWN

I look in the mirror
What do I see?
A damsel in distress
Staring back at me
With eyes so brown
And hair so long
She could be beautiful
But she wears a frown

When you've been raised
With the darkness plain
When you've been blamed
And you feel the shame
When you've been hurt
Screwed to the core
When you know you have
A broken soul
And you're liking it
Getting used to it
And you start wanting more of it
That's when you pray
You begin to crave

Like pouring rain
Pain fall down

She is sadistic
So masochistic
You'd likely think she is
Disturbed or something
She has a smile
Mesmerizing eyes
It hides the fact
That's she's been bludgeoned, brutalized

When you've been raised
With the darkness plain
When you've been blamed
And you feel the shame
When you've been hurt
Screwed to the core
When you know you have
A broken soul
And you're liking it
Getting used to it
And you start wanting more of it
That's when you pray
You begin to crave
Like pouring rain
Pain fall down

19. PAINKILLERS

I didn't imagine I'd be here till now
All my memories dampened in the rain of my tears
I just don't know how I am going to cope with this
Sometimes I find myself on the edge of a precipice

These chains
Painkillers
Erase
Painkillers
They make me feel nothing
A haze
Painkillers
Irate
Painkillers
I don't remember my suffering

For as long as I can recall, I've lived in hell
And I refuse to comprehend it as well
I'm not normal, I'm bruised, I'm a basket case
There's nothing else that can help me anyway

These chains

Painkillers
Slashing
Painkillers
Mutilating
Painkillers
I can't feel anything
Erase
Painkillers
A haze
Painkillers
I don't remember my suffering

20. REMINISCE

Lying here, deep in though
What have I been living for??
Broken dreams, unfulfilled
Always afraid that I might sin
Bowing down to the system
Now my own body faces corruption
And I feel so stone-cold
Like the heart I would have died for

Regrets, self-loathing
I reminisce and I end up grieving
How I could've lived
How much more I could've given
Reminisce, reminisce
One last promised kiss
And I hate this
Let me lie here, die here
Reminisce

Decaying, rotting
The frozen smile on my skeleton
Burning, blazing from my skull

Now my true judgement has begun

Regrets, self-loathing
I reminisce and I end up grieving
How I could've lived
How much more I could've given
Reminisce, reminisce
One last promised kiss
And I hate this
Let me lie here, die here
Reminisce

21. SEX ON THE WEEKEND

She had noticed him a long time ago from across the room
So she reached out to him one day, hoping it wasn't too soon
And from under eager lashes, she asked him out on a date
Hoping he didn't already have someone, that she wasn't too late
And that night when they met, she shyly reached for his hand
But he pulled it away; it wasn't part of his plan
If she was willing to give into him without him having to chase
He could get what he wanted without any time to waste

So he said, "Oh, I think we could just be friends,
I've only got time for sex on the weekend"

He liked romance and fairy tales, but just the ones in books
As far as he knew, people only noticed his looks
And life had betrayed him too many times before
He was always dissatisfied, always wanting more
Yet he was too afraid to try and be himself
His fear of being rejected had him overwhelmed
Even when friends reached out, he acted like he didn't care
He wanted a good love, but he didn't dare

He had a hard time learning to trust, to stay committed
So he played it safe with just sex on the weekend

They had been friends, together for so long
They used to be emotionally intimate, and their bond was so strong
They were safe where they were, and didn't want to take a risk
They loved each other in so many ways, they couldn't resist
Because losing the other would mean the loss of their love
They thought what they had was already enough

They were too scared to settle on a definition
So they drew the line at sex on the weekend

She used to be the life of the party, yet was innocent
And she drowned her issues with alcohol and cigarettes
She had long ago learnt to go with the flow
Because she was too broken to care anymore
And those she loved never felt the same way
Somehow they all managed to walk away
She craved for someone for her to grow old with
To laugh and to talk, and to hold hands with

She eventually became too thick-skinned
So she snorted intimacy with sex on the weekend

He began to want her, more than he thought he would
But she wouldn't hear him, and he felt misunderstood
She felt suffocated, she said, by his proposal
And if it happened again, this would all be over
She had work, she had friends, she had a life outside of him
He had no one, but his heart and his good intentions
And as long as he felt this way about her
He would hold on to hope, and swallow his fear

He wanted more, and he loved her, so he had to pretend
To be fine with just their sex on the weekend

22. SILVER

When I was a child, I saw the world through rose-tinted glasses
A kaleidoscope bursting with hues painted in laughter and innocent truth
The yellow sun lifted in the sky, like the corner of my mother's mouth when she smiled
The apples of her cheeks blushing like ripened fruit

Then in adolescence at school, we learnt about history, science and shapes
Shaped like the boxes we were eager to put things in all the time
A box for pencils, a box for crayons, a box for my exploring mind
But most of all, the teachers insisted we walk and draw within the lines

Then the smoke of the city rose from the edge of my cigarette when I was a teen
It blurred my red eyes, faded my bizarre dreams
The colour of sadness started to ooze in modes of grey on my life's screen
With angry bursts of salamander, green with envy and jealousy

The road I walked, flooded by traffic lights blinking to oncoming

accidents –
The splatter of a shattered heart, the blue stains of fading tears
The day was finally beginning to set on a youth, bright with hopefulness
And I now sit in the silver moonlight, looking back at all those psychedelic years

I wait for the silver shadows to spread across the room, so I can lay down and rest
The dark used to be my friend, now it's my pillow on which I wearily lay my head
My eyes have lost fervour for searching for that silver lining
The only silver that shimmers in the dimness of my life, is silver sprouting on my head

23. SPECIAL NEEDS

I'm handicapped
I'm special needs
It's not that I
Like to smoke weed

It distracts me from the mess
It numbs all of my distress

I'm handicapped
I'm special needs
I need some love
To help me succeed

Right now I've given up all hope
Right now I can't do it anymore

I'm handicapped
I'm special needs
There's an empty hole
When you dig deep

My basic want is to be held

Infinite love can make me well

I'm handicapped
I'm special needs
I'm brokenness
Will I ever heal?

A constant ache in the centre of me
The constant need to please

I'm handicapped
I'm special needs
This fucking disease
Is eating me

Slowly I begin to lose my will
And I do not want to live

I'm handicapped
I'm special needs
I'm everything
You'll never want to be

I'm annoyance, I'm a liability
Excuse me, I'll go get rid of me

24. STATE OF STARVATION

Death!
How sweet and peaceful it must seem
I close my eyes
And wait for its iciness to creep
Slowly engulf this mortal being

See the sad tears streaming down my cheeks
Let their cool water drown the burning within me

The thought that each hour brings me closer to the end
I feel so secure in eternity's well
No more want, no more craving, no more needs to be fulfilled
Just floating in dark waters, slowly sinking in

This is what hunger brings
Hallucinations and a loss of will
Too weak to fight, too cold to think
Just slowly sliding off the brink

25. STEP OUTSIDE

When life is hard and full of sorrow
Knowing it will only get harder tomorrow
When the world bursts forth in its fury
God's love is the epitome of nature's beauty

When all you've wished for comes undone
Step outside, you solemn one
Low and weary are you, mortal creature
Hope is whispered in the serenity of nature

Your own body becomes your prison cell
Close at hand tolls the hopeless knell
Downward cast are your eyes
Find your infinity in the skies

If ever you feel robbed of your power
Note the blossoming of the flower
And when lost for reasons to "Why"
See the uprising of the butterfly

When you have no reason to sing out praise
The trees forever their branches raise

Sometimes obstacles never seem to cease
Feel the strength in the breeze

And when your faith begins to quiver
Immerse yourself in the ever-flowing river
No more fear, no more reason to hide
When you need inspiration, step outside

26. STOP SEXUALIZING ME

When I was a child of 13
My mother pulled me close, sneered at me,
"The only reason your father takes you close to him
Is because you attract him with your big bosom"

When I was a teen of 15
At my school's farewell, I donned a saree
A boy in my class told me, as he salivated,
"I looked at your pictures and I masturbated"

When I was a young lady of 17
Thrown out of the house, living in classroom, rent-free
The boy I clung to, the only person who gave me attention
Stripped me, ripped me, then told me never to mention it

Then I became a woman of 20
Living on my own in my favourite city
Men wanted to have their way with me
And when they were done, they'd stop calling me

It was only after I turned 30
That I began to embrace all of me
I shut the door on those who thought poorly of me
With their small minds and their audacity

Every day, I wake up on my own
Only to survive the day on my own
And when I look in the mirror, I only want to love myself
To live each day wholely, solely for myself

So I face the mirror, try to look my best
Be my best self, live the best
Then someone who has no clue about my story
Thinks they can judge me on the story they wrote for me

I'm not here to interfere
I wish I could disappear
But since I got to do what I can
I request you to just let me do what I planned

Stop sexualizing me
Please, stop sexualizing me
Stop forcing me to believe
That all I'm ever going to be is my body

Don't make me regret
This beautiful body I was blessed with

And a ravishing mind
And a heart that is kind

Maybe you can avert your eyes
Or try looking deep into my eyes
I want to be valued, to be loved for who I AM meant to be
So please, stop sexualizing me

27. THE FLOW

Nothing really is ever still
Not the living heart, not the faltering human will

Like the dance between decisions and the interlope of thoughts
The weaving of destined meetings, the confusion of acquainted tangled knots

The decimation of the present, now the past
The future never reaching, the final destination approaching fast

From the whispering of the breeze betwixt the boughs of trees
To the mumbling rivers and the quivering of the seven seas

The molten heart of the earth, the fleeting cotton clouds
Delicate wings in flight, flickering above living things that abound

Always the arousal of chaos, the skirmish of commotion
The din of beseeching prayer escaping lips, softly in devotion

And in this flow, seldom finding answers to the truths we seek
We acquiesce to the turmoil with inner peace

28. THE HOURS

One day you'll wake up
And the hours would have passed by like a dream
That's when you'll notice
What was an illusion, and what was real
Who was there
When you needed them and when they needed you
Seconds go by and so do days
It's never too late to change your ways
Use each moment to live again
Love again
Fall all over again

29. THERE'S ME

Why can't I be more like everyone else?
I'm by myself on this side of the fence
People don't seem to think that I matter
Everyone looks at me like this pitiful mess

There's me
An obscenity
A thorough misfit
A piece of shit

Those my age have their head in the right place
They know how to say the right things, do what suits them best
They fit in with society, blend in with the rest
Me? I spend my life running from one distraction to the next

There's me
A crime scene
The misplaced sun
The abandoned one

When I look at other people, they have everything to gain
They have their place, they walk a path accepted by the sane

Me? I'm a wreckage no one wants to get dirty with
I've a raw beating heart, but a legacy stained by filth

There's me
An anomaly
A rebellious hymn
A forbidden sin

There are tribes, there are families, there's a circle of friends
People have a sense of belonging somewhere
They have hands to hold and shoulders to lean on
Me? I have my black sheep skin I rely on

There's me
A non-entity
A disgusting reject
A failed experiment

People thrive, they strive as part of life
They can do what it takes to do more than survive
They've a solid head and unwavering mind
Me? I've left my sanity behind

There's me
An oddity
A stray with no name
A family's shame

Anyone will be missed when they're gone
Gone far away, or gone from this world
Someone's heart will break at their irreplaceable loss
Me? I will fade into dust with my cross

There's me
An overlooked obituary
A haphazard human being
The unseen

30. TODAY

Today I've decided to have a ball
To stare into space and do nothing at all

Today I have chosen to put myself first
No emails, no calls to which I will revert

Yesterday, I felt powerless just waiting to get paid
Forgot my purpose, just went with what others said

But creativity doesn't work like that
You need to be free to fly
I will no longer dream on the ground
I will unfurl my mind like the sky

Today I am me, that's only who I'll be
To hell with anyone who tries to stop me

You might ask me what I plan on doing tomorrow
I have no idea, but I won't live it in sorrow

Because today is the day I choose myself
To live wholeheartedly for me, and no one else

31. TRIGGER

Every time I try to let go of fate
It pulls me like a noose around my neck
Anytime I begin to put the pieces back together
My sanity threatens to once again break

Like a fracture that just refuses to heal
My mind keeps reliving all the pain
Everyone is deaf to my silent screams
And I don't want to be the one to complain

I need to stop playing these memories like a movie
Because all it does is act like a trigger
It's lonely inside, where all the demons hide
And all my problems only seem to get bigger

How will this end? Is there a song sad enough?
Do you know of any fast, silent killer?
Maybe the next time I feel myself begin to descend
I will go ahead and pull the trigger

9 798887 838724

Printed by Libri Plureos GmbH in Hamburg,
Germany